GOD SAYS YES 91 TIMES

PROJECT ID-702128

Mary Ardissone

Copyright @2021 Mary Ardissone.

All rights reserved. No part of this book may be used or reproduced by any means, graphic, electronic, or mechanical, including photocopying, recording, taping or by any information storage retrieval system without the written permission of the author except in the case of brief quotations embodied in critical articles and reviews.
Scripture quotations marked NASAB are taken from the
New American Standard Bible R, Copyright 1960, 1962, 1963, 1968, 1971. 1972, 1973, 1975, 1977, 1995 by The Lockman Foundation.
Used by permission.

This book is a work of non-fiction. Unless otherwise noted, the author and the publisher make no explicit guarantees as to the accuracy of the information contained in this book and in some cases, names of people and places have been altered to protect their privacy.

978-1-8383499-6-7 (Hardcover)
978-1-8383938-0-9 (Paperback)
978-1-8383499-7-4 (e-book)

AEGA Design Publishing Ltd
Kemp House, 160 City Road, London
EC1V 2NX, United Kingdom
www.aegadesign.co.uk/ www.aegadesign.com

Because of the dynamic nature of the Internet, any web addresses or links contained in this book may have changed since publication and may no longer be valid. The views expressed in this work are solely those of the author and do not necessarily reflect the views of the publisher, and the publisher hereby disclaims any responsibility for them.

Any people depicted in stock imagery taken from the internet are all copyright free and are for public use for illustrative purposes only.
Library of Congress Control Book: 2017915686

Table of Contents

Section	Page
Introduction	1
Chapter 1	2
Chapter 2	5

-Advertising and Promotion
-Careers
-Celebrities
-Entertainment
-Food
-Health and Medicine
-Inventions/Innovations
-Money/Financial
-Mother Nature
-Politics/Government
-Religion
-Transportation
-Miscellaneous

Chapter 3 .... **49**
-Healing Principles

Chapter 4 .... **52**
-How Do I Pray?

Chapter 5 .... **54**
-Prayer Life Guidelines

Chapter 6 .... **56**
-Spiritual Reflections and Observations

Introduction

As I share with you my prayer experiences where God answered "yes" to the requests, there's the belief that you'll be more hopeful. There's a section at the end of the book for you to write whatever you want to. You may list past requests that were answered "yes," thus affirming the power of prayer. You could list future requests, or simply whatever you feel like writing. Some of you may even write your observations about life.

One of the purposes of this book is to inspire you to remember the various times that your own prayer requests were answered with the answer "yes." It's not easy to cite how often it has happened if we are in a down mood or down on our luck for a period of time. I hope this causes you to remember to write down your past granted prayer requests. It can lift your mood so you can move ahead and not stay stuck where you are.

Some people write down their requests on a regular basis and then put the date of the final response given by God. Keeping a record of requests and recording the final results can be an affirming experience at times.

Some of your requests may require that you personally take action on them to make them happen. In my own life, there were times when prayer and faith alone were enough to make it happen. I hope you have a fulfilling experience.

Chapter 1

Many of us keep our prayer life with God very private, and I've been no exception. Years ago, when I was going through a period of unemployment and financial difficulty, I was upset with God for not bringing in enough money for me to pay my bills on time. At times, I wondered if God was even hearing my prayers. Did He have too much wax in His ears of something? I was trying to be patient for financial relief, but there still wasn't enough coming in. I was getting more upset every day. I wondered if God even cared about me. Did he want me to experience hell on earth or something? I then decided to make a challenge for God. I said, "if you can remind me of many of my significant prayer requests that you answered with 'yes,' I'd write a book about it years later and share the requests with others.

Over the years, I'd write down on scraps of paper anything that I could remember that was answered with "yes." The more I started to remember these and other prayer requests, I simply had to conclude that anything is possible with God. Letting go and letting God is important. Have just enough faith that He'll do it if it's a good idea. What he does with your request may boggle your mind. As I remembered my requests answered with "yes," I started to feel like these truths were stranger than fiction.

One person can make a world of difference. With God, we are all equal in His eyes. He'll do amazing things for anybody. Our prayers are a piece to the puzzle of what makes things happen. Think of it as a tapestry where crude threads show on the back of the quilt. From the front of the tapestry, a beautiful design has taken place that is complete.

God answers our prayer requests with either "yes" or "no" or "wait." Think back upon your prayer requests that were answered with a "yes." Then realize that your desires mattered to God and you are important in His eyes. Just keep those requests coming. He always listens and cares. Some requests may be delayed, but answered with a "yes" nonetheless. Any requests answered with a "no" are simply not in His divine plan for what will be the best situation overall. We grow when God says "no" as well as when He says "yes."

Sometimes we don't understand why our prayer request was answered in a way that was different than what we originally wanted. As time goes on, it may make perfect sense why God answered it as He did. Perhaps we were not personally, spiritually, or professionally ready for our original request to have the best effect in our lives.

As we look back on our lives, if everything we asked for happened, the better things later on would not have happened. If "no" is given, ask what would be a better solution, then go on about your daily life. The answer may come when you least expect it. Are you in a rut? Ask God to inspire you with ideas. God can give <u>anyone</u> a stroke of genius – a great idea or solution. Visualize in the eye of your mind what you want or need. Close your eyes to do it if necessary. Do this often. If you like, sketch a picture of it, or find a picture and refer to it often. Give specific details of what you want or need. Talk in positive terms about it as if it has already happened. Self-talk that is positive is important. Avoid using negative words when talking about or thinking about your request. When you visualize what you want to be, or own, etc., the opportunities will present themselves to make it possible. Ask God for wisdom in what you pray for. An ounce of wisdom is worth a pound of "this is how I get out of this mess!"

Divine help will sometimes come in the form of people without whose talent and dedication we could not succeed. God will do wonderful things through someone who doesn't care who gets the credit. Multiply your intellect and increase your clever abilities by working with others who are more intelligent than you are. Your success becomes possible when you realize you can't do it without others.

There are different types of prayer. Some of the different types are thanksgiving, praise, worship, confession and forgiveness, and petition. This book is about some of the prayer requests that I've prayed over the years that were answered with a "yes." I'm sure that some of them have also benefited you. If you prayed for any of my requests too, then let's face it, there's strength in numbers.

Sometimes my prayer requests for a certain need or desire are very detailed and specific. At other times, the request is prayed for in a more general way. Either method works. You may also ask God for wisdom when making your requests. You can also ask God to modify the results of your request if He has a better idea.

The next section has some prayer requests that I've prayed for over the years that were answered with "yes." The section following that is about intercessory prayer and principles of healing. The final section consists of some reflections and observations that I've made over the years. There's also ample room in the back of the book for you to write about your past and present prayer requests. You may want to include how they are answered eventually. This can be a powerful tool as we reflect on our newest requests.

It will help you to have patience, faith and hope. If your request for a situation to get changed doesn't happen as you want it to, perhaps God wants you to be instrumental in creating a new product, service, relationship, organization, etc. If you personally don't create the solution to the problem, you can always pray for someone else more qualified to do it. So many of the great things that we take for granted started out with our frustration and our search for an answer.

Anything is possible with prayer. Now hold onto your hat as you read about many of my own experiences with prayer requests that were answered with "yes."

Chapter 2
Advertising and Promotion

Westinghouse Logo

Early in my graphic design career, I worked for an engineering company. While looking at one of their drawings, I saw a shape that interested me. It was a "W" with dots on it. I had the idea that it would be an ideal design for a logo. My boss had worked for Westinghouse at one time and it seemed like an ideal design for their logo someday. As time went by, a person designed their logo just the way I had envisioned it.

Staples Logo and Store

There was often a need for me to visit office supply stores. It crossed my mind one day that an office supply such as staples would be an interesting name for such a store. The ideal logo would use an opened metal staple for the "L" in the logo. Eventually, it all took place and there are Staples stores around the country.

Help Wanted Ads

During 1968, I looked for my first full-time job. As I scanned the help wanted ads, it was frustrating to me to see them listed as "help wanted male" and "help wanted female." It didn't make sense to me. Desperate for a job, I answered a "help wanted male" ad for a graphic design technician. During the interview, they seemed puzzled as to why I answered the ad. My portfolio was great they said, so they hired me anyway. I saw it as an important step in helping make equal opportunity happen.

GEICO

At one time, GEICO was a car insurance company that I had an insurance policy with. The creative wheels in my mind started spinning one day when I saw a picture on television for an animal called a gecko. It seemed to be an ideal mascot for their advertising campaigns. As the years went by, it became a popular character in their campaigns. I'm glad someone decided to use it.

CAREERS

President Black Heritage

The office of U.S. President has always been filled by white males. Around 2004, I thought it was about time for a person of black heritage to hold the office if qualified. Several people came to mind, but they weren't interested in the job they said. Finally, as the 2008 election got closer, Barack Obama was a Democratic candidate for the office and he won by a wide margin, just as I had hoped.

US President Barrack Obama

Presidents Central States

Growing up in the Midwest, we were often told that if you want to advance high in a career, move to the East or West Coast. It was almost as if the people in these areas were more intelligent or progressive than the rest of us, or so we were led to believe. I got tired of this attitude so I asked God to make sure that the top job in the country went to people who were originally from, or still living in central or landlocked states. My request was answered yes. Some of the presidents who fit this bill were Lyndon Johnson, Gerald Ford, Jimmy Carter, Ronald Reagan, Bill Clinton, George W. Bush, and Barack Obama.

This picture of the Seal of the United States is a Public Domain picture from Wikipedia

My Writing Career

Around 1989, I was out of work and debating on what direction to take with my career. I had been in the creative field of graphic design for a long time but was willing to consider a change. Writing could be an option, although I wasn't trained in it. Instead of plunging ahead in an unfamiliar area that I may not like or have a talent for, I asked God for a sign that could only come from him. In the Bible, we are told that a camel passing through the eye of a needle was only possible if God did it. So I asked for a similar sign if writing was a good career choice. I proposed to God that a plant grow through the wall of a building. It seemed very unlikely to me until one day I visited the library in Bethesda. I was prompted to look over at the large windows. Lo and behold, several branches of ivy were growing into the room of the library from outside the wall. They managed to grow through the tight crack between the window frame and wall. Needless to say, I got the hint from God.

Carter – Housing

When President Jimmy Carter left office, I thought he'd be useful in the area of housing. When he became involved with Habitat for Humanity, I knew it was a good fit.

Celebrities

Donald Trump

Years ago, I was shopping for books in a bookstore. One stood out in my mind. It was *The Art of the Deal* by Donald Trump. His photo was part of the book as I recall. I didn't know what his financial situation was but asked God to make him super wealthy someday. Today he is a billionaire.

In recent years, I thought that a successful businessman could improve the business and job situation in the United States. My premonition was that if he ran for U.S. President, he would win. He ran for the job of U.S. President and won.

Marriage, Maria Shriver and Arnold Schwarzenegger

When walking to a subway in Washington, D.C. one day, I was thinking about Maria Shriver and her various appearances as a journalist on television. I knew she was single, but wondered who could be an ideal husband for her someday. For reasons I can't explain, the name of Arnold Schwarzenegger entered my mind as a good choice for a husband. Eventually, they married and had children.

Marriage, Kathie Lee and Frank Gifford

On a regular basis, I watched the *Today Show* when I had the morning off. For several mornings, I saw Kathie Lee as a host. A guest was Frank Gifford and the way they related to each other told me there could be a future relationship on the horizon. A chemistry came through on the times they were together on the show. They later married just as I had speculated.

Oprah Winfrey

While living in Baltimore, I watched the news on WJZ-TV with Oprah Winfrey as the co-anchor. After several months, I thought that she could be an ideal choice for a talk show host. The show could feature many topics. She eventually was put in that role for the *People Are Talking* show. It was a hit.

Being a Wisconsin native, I was hoping that a woman who had lived in Milwaukee at one time could host a talk show in Chicago about various topics. The topic of sexual abuse entered my mind as one of many subjects featured on the show. When I thought that Oprah could ideally thrive in a Chicago setting, the prayer went out for her to move and feature her popular show from that location. Later it was learned that she lived in Milwaukee for a while as a child. Over the years, I've watched her show and can see why it was so popular.

As luck would have it, in 1973 I even worked for a short time at WJZ-TV as a graphic artist during a strike. Small world!

Being a billionaire someday was also a hope of mine. She eventually reached that goal too.

This is a representation of a Red Carpet for the Celebrity

Entertainment

MASH

While in college in Minneapolis from 1966 to 1968, the Vietnam War was taking place and was on the news daily. The news was grim. We were getting nowhere fast. To lift the spirits of Americans, I thought a comedy about a war situation would be helpful. It would be about doctors in Korea at a MASH unit. It could start as a movie, then become a popular long-running TV show. Eventually, the movie MASH came out, followed by the television series. It has been so well-received that there are reruns even today.

Our Lady of Good Help

On rare occasions, Jesus mother, the Blessed Virgin Mary, will appear to one or more people for reasons and messages that are special to her. I always wanted her to appear to one or more people in the state of Wisconsin, since I was living there. I often asked her if she would do this. What I didn't realize was that the Vatican would officially recognize her appearances that occurred in 1859 to someone named Adele Brise. Adele became a nun as time went on and taught children the Catholic faith. In 1871, there was the Great Chicago fire. At the same time there was the little known large fire in northeastern Wisconsin by Green Bay. I started in Peshtigo, a lumber village. It leaped across the bay and penetrated Door Peninsula. People gathered in a chapel and prayed that they would be spared. Rain eventually fell. The massive fire was put out through Mary's intercession. The chapel, school and six acres consecrated to Mary were spared from the fire.

This is the only apparition now recognized by the Vatican in the United States. Some miracles have happened since that time.

Jay Leno, The Tonight Show

The *Tonight Show With Johnny Carson* was soon going to need a new permanent host when he left. I watched several hosts appear on the show and felt that Jay Leno was the best choice for that position. As time went on, he was chosen for that role and was a success at it.

Madonna

During the 1980s, I listened to a favorite rock 'n roll station while doing freelance graphic design at a local agency. An upcoming star was named Madonna. When I heard that name, the first thing that came to mind was the Blessed Virgin Mary. She's called the Madonna in the Catholic Church. Her intercession with God has been known to make many great things happen. I asked her to make the singer Madonna very successful in the long run. Her prayers went out and God helped the young singer to become a superstar.

America's Most Wanted TV Show

Television has always been a fast way to get the word out about crimes. I realized that there was a need for a show that would feature profiles and stories about wanted fugitives. An ideal host would be the father of a murdered child, since he'd be able to relate to that theme all too well. The show *America's Most Wanted* started. This helped law enforcement people from around the country catch criminals through the help of television viewers. It was very successful and yet there was a time when it was going to go off the air. Enough people spoke up, including law enforcement people. It remained on and continued to be very helpful.

Saturday Night Fever and Dirty Dancing

During the late 1970s, disco dancing was the craze and the movie *Saturday Night Fever* was at theaters. The movie and music were so well received and I wanted another successful dance and music movie to come out around ten years later. Someone in the heavens heard my request and *Dirty Dancing* came out around 1987. It won awards and the music was also exceptional.

Mary Ardissone

Neil Diamond

I often enjoyed coming up with clever names of products and people. One day, I was thinking about spiritual things. When I prayed at church, I'd often kneel, as did other parishioners. A clever name would be Neil and I'd think about it when kneeling. The most precious of stones is usually considered a diamond. I suddenly had my name in mind for a super special rock 'n roll singer. It was Neil Diamond. His successful career has lasted for many years.

Michael Landon

Bonanza with Michael Landon was a show that was watched regularly by my family when I was growing up. *Little House on the Prairie* was a smash hit too. While still growing up, I had a disturbing premonition about Michael Landon. It concerned his health during his 50's and his problem with cancer. As the years went by, I was worried about him. Eventually, I thought that before he died, it would be ideal for him to play the role of an angel. When *Highway to Heaven* came out, it was a series that was just what I had in mind. It was an ideal role for him before he passed away and went to heaven.

Kathy, Father Knows Best

I used to watch the television series *Father Knows Best* during my childhood. I enjoyed the child actress whose character name was Kathy. Wondering if anyone besides me had been sexually abused, I asked God a question. Was Kathy ever sexually abused too? Decades later, I saw her on the *Hour of Power* television show. On the show, she said she wrote a book about her younger years. She said she too had been sexually abused during her childhood. Thanks, Lauren, for letting me know I wasn't alone during those tender years.

Special Olympics

For years, I watched the Olympic games on television. It crossed my mind one day that people with various disabilities could also have their own Olympic games. I thought that a member of the famous Kennedy family could start this event and run it for years. Eventually, it all took place.

Disneyworld

Going to Disneyworld in California was a childhood wish of mine, but it was very far away from Wisconsin where I was living. I decided that if it was put in Florida, near Orlando, my dad would take me there someday because it would be closer. I realized that if Walt Disney made a public announcement about his plans, people would buy vacant land there and sell it to him at too high a price for him to afford. One of my solutions was that Walt Disney have some friends buy land in Florida and keep its future use a secret. The land would then be sold to Walt Disney at a reasonable price so he could carry out his plans for Disneyworld. Decades later, I read an article that said the transactions took place that way. Even kids can have good ideas sometimes.

Green Bay Packers

I enjoyed watching the Green Bay Packers football team when I was growing up. They had some fantastic players. During my early teens, I had an idea. Why couldn't someone invent a game called the Super Bowl with the two best teams competing. Several years later, the first Super Bowl took place. Part of my prayer request was that the Green Bay Packers would win the championship the first two years. It took place.

In the early 1990s, I knew I'd move from Maryland back to Wisconsin someday. At the end of 1992, I moved to Watertown to be close to some of my family members. I had prayed that the Green Bay Packers would win again in around five years. They won the Super Bowl in 1997, decades after their first two victories.

Candid Camera

Years ago, I watched *Candid Camera*. It was funny to watch people being caught off guard in humorous situations. I was actually hoping I could be on the show someday. If that didn't happen, I wanted to meet two people who were on *Candid Camera*. I eventually met the two people. The first one was my former husband Frank. As a child, he said he was acting in a scene of a play with a well-known actor. He was supposed to light a torch, but it wasn't able to happen. His quick thinking caused him to say that, although the torch didn't light the light, the flame was in our hearts.

Mary Ardissone

The next person on *Candid Camera* was Phyllis, a woman in the Washington, D.C. area that I rented a room from on a temporary basis. She told me her story. While her husband was away on a business trip, a family pulled up to her house. The father said that he was a good friend of her husband's. Her husband said the family could stay at the house while visiting the area. Phyllis said her husband never mentioned it and she was reluctant to let them stay with her while he was gone. The man persisted for awhile. Eventually, he said she was on *Candid Camera* and her husband was aware of the visit before he left on his trip. She laughed when she found out about the joke that had been played on her.

A Movie Camera

Beatles

When I was a young teen, it was 1962. On a regular basis, I listened to rock 'n roll music, but got tired of the same old styles of songs being put out. Change was needed. I was wearing a very large ladybug scatter pin one day and thought that an interesting name for a singing group would be the name of a bug. I tossed several ideas around in my mind and eventually settled on the name beetles, but it would be spelled Beatles.

The desire was that they be English, have a new style of singing, and be world famous someday. A couple of years later, it took place as I had hoped.

After they had been around a few years, I had an idea for a song. The words and melody went through my mind. The song was called, *Let It Be*. I requested that the Blessed Virgin Mary be instrumental in making it happen through her prayers. I chose the Beatles as an ideal group to put out the song. Paul McCartney eventually sang the song and it's played on the radio even today.

When I hear the words, "let it be," two interpretations come to mind. One of them is, so be it. The other is, leave the situation alone for now. When I hear the song, I often sense which interpretation I should pay attention to at the time.

The Beatles

Food

Wendy's

Hamburgers were always a favorite of mine. I'm often interested in new things, and one day I got an idea for a name of a chain of hamburger restaurants. Peter Pan's story gave me the idea for the name of Wendy. It seemed ideal at the time. Square hamburgers would mean less wasted meat. The logo that was envisioned was a girl with red hair and braids. The style of lettering of the logo would be in a style typical of that in the old Western publications. Dave Thomas started this restaurant chain with details as I had envisioned them. He even was a supporter of causes for adopted children, which at the time sounded like a good direction for him to take someday.

McDonald's

I grew up in a town near Madison, Wisconsin. My dad would sometimes take us kids along on business trips. I was around nine at the time. For dinner one day, he suggested that we try a restaurant with two large arches as part of the building design. It was called McDonald's. I enjoyed their hamburgers so much that I wanted one close to areas I moved to as I got older. I got home and played the song *Old McDonald Had a Farm* and thought about the restaurant. Two yellow rainbows to form the letter "M" seemed like a great design for them as a logo. It all took place as the years went by and the corporate headquarters was in Illinois, which seemed like a good choice to me at the time.

God Says Yes 91 Times

This represents a fast food product

HEALTH AND MEDICINE

Cameras in the Body

I realized that finding problems in the body couldn't always be seen best by x-rays. There was a better way I knew. So why not put a camera at the end of a tube and insert it into the holes of the body? Eventually, the experts found a way to do it.

Jerry Lewis and MD

Dean Martin and Jerry Lewis were often watched by my brothers, sisters, and myself on television. They were both successful, and one day I thought that Jerry Lewis could do something helpful for a charity. I heard of the disease called Muscular Dystrophy, but knew little about it. Nonetheless, I asked God to prompt him to take up the cause as a fundraiser. Eventually, he did and has been successful doing it ever since.

Danny Thomas

Make Room for Daddy was a show I often watched years ago. It starred Danny Thomas. I knew that sick children could benefit from a crusader and he crossed my mind as a good choice for that type of work. I asked God if he would help create a hospital for sick children. When St. Jude Children's Research Hospital started up, I knew he was doing a great service for children.

Cut Slits for Operations

Surgery usually involved much cutting of tissue and muscle to get to the organs to be operated on. I thought there must be a better way. Why not cut slits and pull out the desired tissues and organ? Years later, I watched a doctor on television discuss how he was able to perform gallbladder surgery without the usual amount of cutting. It was a great step forward in medicine.

Depicts International Symbol for Medicine

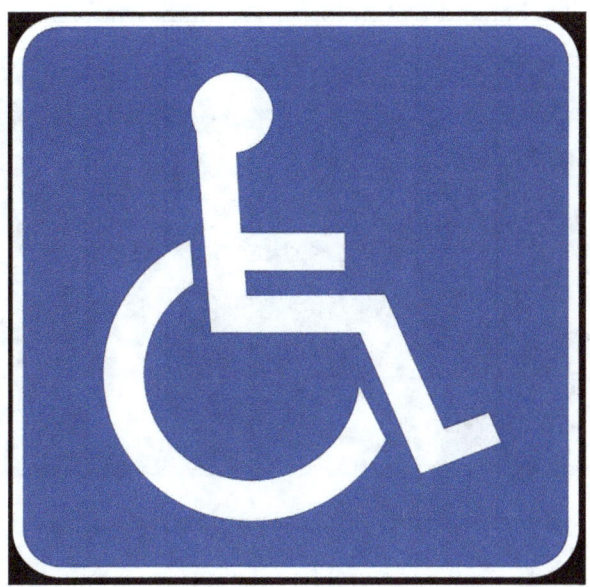

The International Symbol for Wheelchair

Inventions/Innovations

Personal Computers

*F*or years, computers were very large machines. I knew there had to be a better way. I saw, in the eye of my mind, what a small tabletop personal computer would look like. I asked God to find an inventor in California to create this. It would have a keyboard, a moving arrow on the screen, and a gadget called a mouse with a cord on it. The company he would create would be called Apple with the logo having a bite taken out of the apple. God selected Steve Jobs for this invention and the rest is computer history. It really changed technology in so many ways.

A presentation of the Interior part of a laptop

Polaroid

When I worked in the camera department of a large store, I heard that Polaroid was suing Kodak for patent infringement on their camera. I prayed that Polaroid would win the case and they did.

Carbonless Paper

Years ago, carbon paper was put between two sheets of paper when you needed two or more copies of a form. It would make a dark smudge on your fingers if you weren't careful when handling it. I knew there had to be a better way to make duplicate copies. An idea occurred to me one day. Why not coat the backside of a form with a speckled coating that would transfer to the paper below when pressure was applied? Years later, someone invented it and I often used it for business purposes.

B2-Stealth Jet

When working for a government contractor, I was looking through a book of logos. One design caught my eye. The design was circular in nature with a shape in the circle. I divided the shape into fourths. It then looked to me like an ideal shape for a modern jet. I thought that it could have a design and coating that could make it hard to detect by radar. Years later, the B2-Stealth Jet was introduced. They said the design was put into place a number of years ago, but no one had considered it too seriously. Today, its military use is very useful in difficult situations.

B-52 Fighter Jet

Mary Ardissone

Seatbelts

During the later 1950s, I was riding in the backseat of a friend's car. The driver slammed on the brakes. I hit the front seat but escaped serious injury. Realizing the seriousness of the situation, I thought someone should invent seatbelts so people could escape serious injury in many accidents. Eventually, they became a standard feature in all cars.

Airbag

As the years went by, I thought that a new feature could be added to cars so that people avoid being seriously injured. The concept of the airbag occurred to me. I was glad when someone finally invented it and it became a necessity in all new cars.

Dupont Telfon

It was frustrating to scrub burnt-on food from pots and pans years ago. Someone needed to come up with a coating to make clean-up easier. I thought that Dupont would be a good company to handle this need. Eventually, they introduced a Teflon coating for pots and pans and it helped solve the problem.

Barbie Doll

I played with teenage dolls as a little girl and had a vision for a new doll. She'd be more slender, have blond hair and her name would be Barbie. Her popularity for generations was a desire of mine too. My wish was in the late 1950s and she still is enjoyed by little girls today, 50 years later.

Suitcases on Wheels

When I'd fly home to Wisconsin from Maryland, it seemed as though my heavy suitcase was too hard to carry long distances. There was a vision in my mind for someone to put wheels on suitcases. Thank goodness it finally happened.

3M Post-it Notes

As a graphic artist, I saw a need. When I'd present artwork and pasted up text copy to supervisors or clients, they'd mark up the original material.

Sometimes the artwork needed to be redone because of their notations. I wanted a company to invent a piece of paper with a coating on the back of it. The coating would stick to paper, but not harm the surface. To me, 3M was an ideal choice for this invention since they handled adhesives on tapes. The idea I thought could be the result of a mistake or problem they'd have trying to create another kind of adhesive. Years later, I read that the invention came about just that way. Today, I use it for all kinds of purposes, marking things on paper and using them for bookmarks too.

Microwave Ovens

When I dated a sailor in the late 1960s, we were talking about a number of things. The subject of microwaves came up. I wasn't familiar with them and he explained it to me. He said he'd heard of a guy injured by them. I asked him how someone could get hurt by microwaves. He explained that, if you were hit by microwaves, you would get cooked inside. At that moment, I had an idea. Why not create a microwave oven for cooking food? Years later, it happened and most kitchens have one. It speeds up cooking time and fewer dishes get dirty when cooking or reheating food.

Mary Ardissone

Xerox Machines

In the 1950s and early 1960s, I often wanted to make a duplicate copy of something. I was told that I would out of luck. Perhaps a company could invent a copying machine. That would solve the problem I thought. The company's name could begin with an "X" since that was an uncommon letter for a first name of a company. As time went on, Xerox came out with a copying machine and I was one happy gal.

White Correction Fluid

Years ago, when I'd make a mistake typing something, I had to use a special eraser to try to remove the type. With pen and ink artwork, sometimes I'd use a fine blade to scrape away ink lines. There had to be a better way. A white correction fluid would be a possible solution and you could type and draw over it when it was dry. Not knowing who could invent this, a thought crossed my mind. Why not have a frustrated office worker come up with a concoction in her home? The singing group called the Monkees was a favorite of mine. Perhaps one of them had a mother who would fit this bill. When the invention came out, I was grateful. Years later, I heard on a television program that a mother of one of the Monkees created the product and became rich in the process. Pretty amazing!

Pop-top Cans

In the mid 1960s, I had to use a bottle opener to make an opening in the top of a soda can. It was inconvenient. The can was less portable since a bottle opener always had to be nearby. One day, I had an idea for a seamless pop-top can. I didn't know how to invent it, but wanted to meet someone within a few years who was working on the invention. While attending college, I met a graphic design student names Dennis. He was making patent drawings of that concept for his father and uncle. I gave him my input on the metal part that would pop out. Years later, the pop-top can became a standard on cans. Another desire fulfilled.

Bathroom Needs

During the 1950's, and 1960's, I'd get desperate at an outdoor event if I needed to use a toilet but there wasn't one in sight. Someone, I thought, needed to invent a portable toilet for public events. Years later, they finally came out.

At airports and other public restrooms, women had to hunt for coins before they could unlock the doors to toilets in the bathroom. If you were out of the right change, you had to find someone who had the correct change. The whole situation was ridiculous and inconvenient to say the least. Bathrooms should be free. I made a prayer request that the situation change from pay toilets to free ones. Thanks goodness it eventually happened.

Another irritating situation in a public restroom was having little or no toilet paper when you really needed it. I wanted someone to create very large rolls of toilet paper to solve the problem. Eventually, they came out and many desperate people were relieved.

Computers for Handicapped

While working at a newspaper one day, an article and photo came up about a man who was paralyzed from the neck down. This kind of disability was probably difficult to live with. There was the premonition that someone close to me would have that problem someday and would need advances in computer technology to make life easier and more productive. My brother Bill's name entered my mind. Before anything would happen to him, I had some ideas in mind. There could be a microphone that he could speak into and words would appear on the screen. A roller ball on a mouse could help him move the arrow on the screen. Other advances could also come out before his problem occurred. The premonition came around 1986. Bill's car accident occurred around 1998. The advances in technology certainly made his life easier and the use of the computer made it possible for him to take on interesting projects.

There was also the idea that computer chips could be put into artificial limbs to help them move naturally. Eventually, that took place.

Gillette Good News Razors

It was frustrating to use the older razor blades. Unless they were adjusted correctly, they'd make cuts on your skin. I had that problem myself and knew that one pass of the razor on my skin still left more hair than I had hoped for. There had to be a better way. Then I thought two blades close together were better than one. The razor's blades could be already installed at a good angle so that you didn't insert razor blades into the razor yourself. It was a safe solution. When Gillette came out with that kind of razor and called it the Good News Razor, it was good news to me.

Money/Financial

Glenn – Lottery

While in high school, I always wanted to get more dates. I wasn't, however, a cheerleader, class president, or one of the most popular girls.

My girlfriends and I would go to a small restaurant after sports events. There was a young man names Glenn who worked at the grill, and often waited on tables. He'd flirt with me and smile consistently. It lifted my spirits when my dating life was going nowhere. Over the years, I never forgot these kind gestures and wanted to show my thanks to him in some secret way. It seemed that one way was to reward him financially. When Wisconsin eventually had a lottery, this seemed like an ideal solution. I asked God to let him win $100,000 in the lottery. I knew it could make him very happy. As the years went by, he won that amount in the lottery.

Represents a happy person with lots of money after winning a lottery

Dunkin Donuts – Lottery

While living in Maryland in the 1970s, the state started a lottery. When I heard the news, I thought it would be great if an average laborer could win the first million dollars. While driving past a Dunkin Donuts eatery, I thought perhaps an employee from that company could be the first winner. Time went by, and I didn't think much more about it. Then one day, I was with a friend eating at Dunkin Donuts. There was a photographer shooting pictures of a man in the back room who was making donuts. When asking the waitress what was going on, she said he'd won a million dollars in the lottery and was interested in going back to work for them again. Amazing!

Dad's Bookkeeper

My dad had a highway landscaping business and used the services of a bookkeeper. One day, my dad took me to visit the bookkeeper. I felt uneasy around this man. It crossed my mind that he was probably stealing money from my dad's business. It was clear to me that I had no proof and who would believe a kid on such a matter anyway. I asked God to have a trusted employee discover the problem. Years later, a woman that worked for my dad discovered what was going on and the bookkeeper stopped working for my dad.

Bill Gates

While living in the Washington, D.C. area, I decided to attend a trade show with computer companies from around the country attending. I wasn't too familiar with computers at the time. I went by a display that had the Microsoft Windows logo on it. It occurred to me that when you look out the window, you see the heavens. With heaven, all things are possible. I listened intently to a man discussing the Windows product. I thought he was just another salesman. I looked at his face with interest. It crossed my mind that just maybe he could be the richest man in the world with God's help, so I asked for the favor. Years later, I saw this man in an article about Microsoft. This man, Bill Gates, had eventually become the world's richest man.

Mother Nature

Mount St. Helens

During the year 1980, I heard that Mount St. Helen would someday erupt, but the experts weren't sure when it would happen. One day, a date entered my mind as the possible date it would erupt. I had a friend, Orlan, who lived in Oregon. I thought he'd consider this to be a once-in-a-lifetime experience if he saw it erupt. A prayer was said that on a certain date he'd be near the mountain as it blew its stack. When he witnessed it, he said it was something amazing that he'd never forget.

Tornado/Meteor Court

I had never witnessed a tornado before and wondered what it would be like to be near one. While living on Meteor Court in Baltimore in the 1970s, the opportunity would soon happen. Three days before it occurred, I knew it was coming, I hoped it wouldn't touch down and cause much damage. It happened on schedule and took the rooftops off some apartment buildings a few blocks away. It didn't touch down, however, and damage was kept to a minimum and people escaped the buildings just in time.

God Says Yes 91 Times

This is only a representation of a Tornado

Silent Spring/Pollution

During my 11th year, I noticed a puddle of oil on the grass. I saw it as a form of pollution. In my town, trucks would turn on the fog of a mosquito spray around the area too. I nearly gagged. I wanted a woman to write an important book about pollution in the next few years. It could change the attitude of many people I thought. In 1962, when Rachel Carson's book *Silent Spring* came out, pesticides were considered part of the pollution problem. The country's mind started to change for the better on this important subject.

Earthquake, San Francisco

Around 1987, while working on a map as a cartographer, a disturbing vision came into my mind. It was one of an elevated road collapsing. San Francisco was the first city that entered my mind. I saw it as one causing much damage. It would also cause much injury if too many people were on the roadway at the time. Since the date of October 18, 1989 came into my mind, I realized that one way to keep people off that roadway at that time of year was to have a World Series game in San Francisco. Since many people would be glued to their televisions and in the stadium during the earthquake, fewer deaths would result, or so I figured. I prayed for the San Francisco team to be in the World Series that year, and they eventually were. When the earthquake struck that day, injuries and deaths were kept down, thank goodness.

This is representation of an act of nature - a volcano eruption

Politics/Government

Bushes President U.S.

In the 1990s, I thought it could be a good idea to have two closely related people serve as the President of the United States. I was open-minded on which party they'd be from. Their identity was open to me too. During the 2000 presidential election, this took place as George W. Bush became President several years after his father served as President.

The White House

Mary Ardissone

JFK Presidency

I grew up in Watertown, a small town in Wisconsin. When the 1960 presidential election got closer, I prayed that someday I could meet the Senator who would win the election. I was also asking that he have a family member who lived close to me. The reason for that was because I thought maybe I could meet the senator while he was visiting a family member. As time went by, I briefly met Senator John Kennedy. He was visiting a sister in Ft. Atkinson, which was a half-hour away from where I lived. He was in a restaurant with other family members.

2000 Presidential Election

For years, I was considering running for some public office. Before I would do it, however, I wanted to know if the election process had any problems that needed to get worked out. I prayed that the 2000 presidential election would point out any problems that needed to be worked on. The election of 2000 was historic to say the least. Hanging chads on the cards, pleas from the people to get the courts involved were part of the process. The winner couldn't be declared for a while either. I guess I got the answer that there were indeed some problems to be straightened out. Eventually, some of the problems of casting ballots were addressed and, hopefully, some of the issues worked out for the better.

Religion

Charles Colson/Ministry

When people of President Nixon's Administration went to prison, one of them was Charles Colson. I knew he had great potential when he got out. It was clear that when he got his life right with God, he could successfully start a ministry that helped prisoners. He eventually started the Prison Fellowship ministry and it has helped many people. I thought it was a smart career move. Years later, I visited the organization when I interviewed for work as a graphic artist.

St. Pope John Paul II

For centuries, the Catholic Church's cardinals had been electing a pope from Italy. It was clear to me it was time for a change. A prayer was said that the next pope would be from a communist country. When St. Pope John Paul II from Poland was selected, I was overjoyed. After he had been in office for a number of years, I had a premonition that someone would shoot him someday, but I wanted him to survive and thank the Blessed Virgin Mary for helping to protect him from a fatal shooting. He survived the wounds and thanked Mother Mary for helping him to live through it.

Dream Team

When it came to changing communist countries to democracies, I had an idea. I selected a dream team of three men to work as a group to help it take place. It would be the U.S. President Ronald Reagan, St. Pope John Paul II, and the head of the CIA. A flurry of activities took place behind the scenes I was told, and kept secret from the public. They finally accomplished what took decades to accomplish. Democracy took place in many communist countries.

Mary Ardissone

"This is a representation of the Dream Team"

Saint Mother Teresa of Calcutta

As a child, I wondered if there were many Christians in India. If there weren't, perhaps a nun could make a difference among the poor. I wanted one to become prominent over the years and help that cause. When Mother Teresa became a household name, she was the best choice as far as I was concerned. She became a canonized saint, which is a privilege given to few people.

Nuns Without Habits

My Catholic school education left me wondering if the nuns that taught me would always be required to wear the black and white habits. I certainly wanted to see my favorite nun, Sister Rita Ann, in street clothes and without a veil someday. Over the years, the order of nuns that she belonged to changed from black and white habits to regular street clothes. Many years later, when I was at a meeting, I met Sister Rita Ann in street clothes and without a habit. The childhood prayer was answered with a "yes."

Medjugorje Mother Mary

During my Catholic education, there was mention of two apparitions of the Blessed Virgin Mary to children in Fatima, Portugal, and Lourdes, France. Miracles of healing would take place there among the millions of tourists that would visit both shrines. I always wanted a modern day event to take place like these since they happened long ago.

In my younger years, I prayed and asked for that kind of event to happen to me when I got older. The country could be communist, such as Yugoslavia, since that country had a more lenient form of communism, or so I thought. It would happen to children again was the assumption.

During the 1980s, there was an opportunity for me to join a group that visited foreign embassies in Washington, D.C. We'd visit various ones and they'd discuss topics about their country. At the Yugoslavian Embassy, they discussed tourism. During their presentation, a thought entered my mind. The thought was that the apparitions of the Blessed Virgin Mary would happen soon and bring in many tourists to that country on a regular basis for years.

It took place shortly after that, and books were also written about the visitations and various miracles that had been taking place.

Someday I wanted to visit the town of Medjugorje and visit the shrine too. During a period of unemployment, the money came into my life to make the trip with a small group. My desire was that the weather be pleasant with flowers blooming. When we arrived earlier in the year, flowers were blooming everywhere, which they said was unusual for that time of year. I enjoyed the trip and some inner healing of emotions took place.

Robert H. Schuller

As a child, I'd get bored with many sermons I listened to. Sometimes they were hell, fire, and brimstone. Sometimes they emphasized what big sinners we all were. I wanted a better experience in my Christian walk with God. Prayers were said for a minister to come from Iowa to start a more positive mental attitude ministry in California. I chose Iowa because it was next to Wisconsin. A name for the television service entered my mind. It was the *Hour of Power*.

Years went by, and during the early 1980s, I saw the *Hour of Power* show with Robert H. Schuller. The services were positive and just what I had in mind. He was a fan of Bishop Fulton Sheen's television programs as was I. He was also from Iowa. He wrote positive attitude books and tapes, which I bought and listened to. The approach was ecumenical, which was a breath of fresh air since many denominations would put each other's beliefs down.

During the late 1980s, when I lost my job, I desperately wanted to meet him since I was a big fan of his. As luck would have it, I heard he and his son Robert were visiting Baltimore on a book-signing tour. It was only about 35 miles from where I was living in the Washington, D.C. area. I rushed over to the bookstore one day and was first to arrive. I bought a book from both Dr. Robert H. Schuller and his son Robert. I explained my job loss situation and they prayed with me to have the situation turn out well in the long run. It was a boost to my morale when I needed it most.

Our Lady of Good Help

On rare occasions, Jesus's mother, the Blessed Virgin Mary, will appear to one or more people for reasons and messages that are special to her. I always wanted her to appear to one or more people in the state of Wisconsin since I was living there. I often asked her if she would do this. What I didn't realize was that the Vatican would officially recognize her appearances that occurred in 1859 to someone named Adele Brise. Adele became a nun as time went on and taught children the Catholic faith. In

1871, there was the Great Chicago fire. At the same time, there was a little known large fire in northeastern Wisconsin by Green Bay. It started in Peshtigo, a lumber village. It leaped across the bay and penetrated Door Peninsula. People gathered in a chapel and prayed that they would be spared. Rain eventually fell. The massive fire was put out through Mary's intercession. The chapel, school and six acres consecrated to Mary were spared from the fire.

This is the only apparition now recognized by the Vatican in the United States. Some miracles have happened there since that time.

Transportation

Interstate Highway System

As a child riding from town to town, it sure seemed like there were quite a few stoplights. I wanted many highways built without traffic lights. The assumption was that a project like that could take an act of President Eisenhower to make it happen. He eventually endorsed the interstate highway system for military reasons, or so he said. My desire was only to travel long distances without many traffic lights and also to provide my dad with many years of profitable work. My dad's business mushroomed when the interstate highways in Wisconsin needed landscaping. He was also able to provide a good standard of living for our large family.

Trailer Bars on Trailer Trucks

While living in Baltimore, I occasionally dated a guy who had an accident with a tractor-trailer. His car had a low roof and he slide under the trailer, nearly escaping serious injury. I then realized that what trailers needed was a bar behind the trailer to stop cars from sliding under them. As the years went by, semi-tractor-trailers had this feature.

Round Roofs on Semi's

When I saw semi's pulling trailers years ago, it seemed like there was poor airflow from the trucks to the trailers. This drag would eat up more gasoline. I realized that someone needed to invent semis with an elevated rounded roof. It would provide better airflow over the top of the trucks and save gas too. Eventually, someone decided that the idea made sense. Today, it's a common feature on trucks.

God Says Yes 91 Times

Toyotas

During the mid 1970s, I worked with a woman who owned a Toyota. She said it ran well and seldom needed repairs. I realized that the American consumer needed many of these well-designed and great operating cars. My prayer went out. People that I met over the years all had good compliments to say about their Toyotas. Today, they're a giant force in the U.S. auto industry.

Miscellaneous

Parachute Incident

For years, I always wanted to meet someone who had the chance to survive parachute failure. In the mid-1970s, I met Eric who had that experience while in the military. When he jumped, neither of his parachutes opened up. He had been trained to curl up into a ball when falling. He aimed his body to an opening in a wooded area. He landed one foot first into a mud hole and did a spin-around. Amazingly, he survived with only a broken foot. He said he was thankful to God for saving his life. It wasn't his time to die, he said.

This illustrates a man standing still after landing with his parachute

Missing Children Postcards

Like most people, it was disturbing to me to find out that another child had been kidnapped and was still missing. It seemed to be as hard as finding a needle in a haystack to recover the child. Getting the word out to as many people as possible would be helpful, I assumed. A solution crossed my mind. Create postcards advertising products and services with a missing child photo and information on one side of the card. Eventually, they were created and I had the chance to do freelance graphic design for a company that was doing it in the Columbia, Maryland area.

Fire Department Ambulances

When growing up in the 1950s, and 1960s, it was very common for a funeral home to go to an accident site to help the injured get fast medical attention. An article I was reading said it wasn't uncommon for some funeral homes to abuse this service. It said that some of them would help those less seriously injured first. The more critically injured people were helped last or left to die. It was a surefire way to get a new customer, they thought. I realized that helping people in serious need such as this required a public service of a fire department. Profit wouldn't be their motive. Thank goodness the change happened and it became a standard service in communities all over the country.

Another way to rescue people in need also crossed my mind in the early 1970s. Why not have helicopters fly to accident scenes to rescue people quickly and get them to hospitals without delay? I thought that retired Vietnam veteran pilots could be ideal for this service. Eventually, Maryland, where I was living at the time, started this service.

Linda – Red Ball

While driving from Maryland to Wisconsin, a moving van caught my eye. It was the Red Ball Moving Company in Seattle. I had a sister, Linda, who lived in Seattle. Perhaps she could work for them someday if she needed a job. In a few years, when she was job hunting, she landed a job with them and worked with the top executive for a number of years.

Mary Ardissone

Ziggy

A favorite cartoon character of mine was Ziggy. Over the years, I enjoyed him in the newspaper. For reasons I can't explain, I thought that perhaps the artist who created him could make a minimum of a million dollars if the right opportunity ever presented itself.

When I was interviewing with a government agency for freelance graphics work, I met a friend of the creator of Ziggy. We got to talking and he mentioned that his friend had made a seven-figure sum with his famous character Ziggy. Way to go!

Oilman Scholarships

When working for a petroleum trade association in the early 1980s, I saw firsthand how prosperous many of its members had become. One way that a prosperous oilman could give back to the community was to help needy children. He'd offer scholarships for college to deserving students with good grade averages. The students had conditions that had to be met, he said. They couldn't drink or go on drugs. They couldn't get pregnant. It gave the students an incentive to stay well-behaved. On television years later, I saw a story about an oilman in Louisiana who started this project with much success.

Doris – Prudential

I'd buy shoes in the 1950s and 1960s from a nice saleswoman named Doris at a local shoe store. I thought she'd be talented enough to possibly sell insurance someday. When she knew her job situation had to change, she wasn't certain what was the best direction to take. In the meantime, I saw a Prudential commercial on television and thought she's make a good fit in that company. Eventually, she joined them and became a very successful salesperson.

Amway – LOC

As a girl scout in Wisconsin, we took a trip on a clipper ship across Lake Michigan to Muskegon, Michigan. After we returned, I thought that perhaps some men from Michigan could create a company that invented cleaning products. Since people in the United States are always looking for chances to start up new companies, this seemed to be an ideal opportunity and the American way. My name of this new company would be Amway (short for American way). One of their first products could be a cleaning solution called LOC. In my mind, as a child, that meant it could clean up "lots of crud." The business and product eventually took off successfully. Years later, I became an Amway distributor for a few years and met some millionaire distributors. My career path took me to other areas of interest, but I saw products that were good quality and saw a good business opportunity for a number of people.

UMBC Job

For years, I always wanted to work as a graphic designer for a university, but didn't' see the opportunity just yet. Then one day, I lost my job. Not knowing where to turn, I scanned the want ads. Three weeks later, I noticed a job for an illustrator at a local university. I sent in a resume and had a portfolio review. During the job interview, the professor said the job was newly created and they were excited about being able to have the service on campus, rather than sending it out to be done. They hired me and I got my wish.

Wal Mart

I always liked the idea of a department store that sold numerous lines of products. It could be one-stop shopping. One day, a person's last name crossed my mind. The name was Walton. Perhaps he'd be from a southern state. The name of the store could be one that used part of his last name. It could also become a retail giant someday. When Wal Mart started and exploded in growth, it met a need for less expensive products in all categories. As it turned out, the headquarters was also in a southern state.

Curves

The idea of a new exercise franchise chain was a good idea, I thought. Perhaps it could have an exercise routine that was half-an-hour long. The routine could consist of walking in place for 30 seconds, then using an exercise machine for 30 seconds. The routine would continue with this cycle of switching from walking to an exercise machine. This idea could even be heaven sent, I thought. Several years later, a franchise called Curves was started. The founder's name was even Gary Heaven. I also joined for several years.

Sue's Husband

I was riding along with a friend from church. Suddenly, a disturbing feeling came over me. It was about her husband who I had never met. I felt alerted that, in about two weeks, he'd pass away from a heart attack. I knew my friend would be upset if the last week wasn't made special for him in various ways. At the time, she wasn't aware that he would die at the end of the two weeks. He passed away at the end of the week that she had made especially nice for him. She told me about it months later. I didn't confide in her about the heavenly warning that I had received.

100 Year-old Celebrities

Rose Kennedy and George Burns were special people that many people admired. In my younger years, I wanted them to live to be centurions before passing away. Both of them reached at least 100 years.

Dad – Ohio Threat

My dad owned a landscaping business, and during my childhood, he decided to do some work in Ohio. Some competitors in Ohio didn't like the idea, and threatened his life if he did the work. Back in Wisconsin, I was visiting with one of his employees and they casually mentioned the situation to me. I got very worried and immediately prayed for God to keep him safe while he did the work in Ohio. He stayed safe, thank goodness. Many years later, the subject came up during my conversation with him. He said that when he was young, he was naïve about this threat from these specific kinds of people. He felt lucky to be alive.

Harvey Wallbanger

During the 1970s, one drink I occasionally tried was called a Harvey Wallbanger. A brainstorm came to my mind one day. Banking machines outside a bank building were starting up. Why not have a local bank chain call this machine a Harvey Wallbanker? Several years later, they did.

Adopt-a-Highway Program

While living in Maryland, I noticed that highways had quite a bit of litter. Other states had similar problems. Why not have local groups from various organizations pick up litter from a stretch of highway every so often. A sign would be put up that acknowledged what they were doing. The program later started in Maryland and spread to other states too.

Outlet Mall, Johnson's Creek

The two largest cities in Wisconsin are Milwaukee and Madison. They are about 80 miles apart. While living a few miles from the village of Johnson's Creek, I saw a need. The village was centrally located between the two largest cities and needed a boost to its economy. It would also be a great idea to have an outlet mall there to draw people in from both Madison and Milwaukee. A few years later, an outlet mall was built and a few large stores opened up too. Landowners sold their land and some became millionaires, including a friend of my family.

Tammy Lee and Jim Baker

During the 1980s, I was out of work and watching a religious television program one day. Their only focus was raising money and not preaching about God. This went on for several weeks. I questioned the direction that their ministry had taken if money was their main focus. I asked God to let me know if the financial affairs of their ministry needed to be investigated. Within a few months, the money problems came to light and Jim Baker served jail time.

FBI – Fugitive – Murderer

On the news one day, they reported that a father had murdered his children and wife. Authorities didn't have any luck finding him for a long time. One day, his story was retold on television and I sensed that the time was right for him to be found and prosecuted. His story could also be featured on the *America's Most Wanted* television show. An artist would be able to

Mary Ardissone

design a sculpture of his head the way he's probably look years later. That all happened and he was found. The state that he'd be found in crossed my mind once, but I was open-minded about how it would be solved. It was solved by the use of the sculpture. I also prayed that his head would be featured in the exhibit at the FBI building in Washington, D.C. Years later, I went on a tour of that building and there was a sculpture of his head on display.

Chapter 3
Healing Principles

*F*aith that a prayer request will be answered with "yes" can be a helpful tool in getting that response. We believe that God has granted the request, based on listening to him. We then pray for completion and fulfillment of it. We, in essence, are praying for something that has already been granted. Praising and thanking God is a crucial part of prayer life. No matter what answer we receive to our request, thanking God shows our acknowledgement that his wisdom on how to handle the situation is better than ours. Many of our prayer requests that we've forgotten about are often answered by a new request being answered with "no." Example: You don't get a desired job. As a result of a different job, you may get better terms, salary, hours, new friends you value, more free time to do things you always wanted to do, etc. These new things may be older prayer requests you've forgotten about.

Faith is an important element. It is a gift rather than more strenuous will power. It isn't wishful thinking. Faith is the confident assurance of things hoped for, and conviction about things we do not see. It is a gift and the conviction and certainty comes to us only by the grace of God. You can pray for it.

Who needs the faith for the request to be granted? The faith may be that of the recipient of the request. Faith may be in the intercessor. Faith may be on behalf of someone else. For example, in Matthew 9 and Mark 2, it says that Jesus healed by responding to the faith of those who brought the paralytic to him.

Pray for faith, which is infused with certainty and confidence.

Pray for wisdom on what to pray for. God may want you to tone down your request at this phase of your life. He may also want you to take a big leap of faith and expect a great deal more than you originally expected.

If you believe that God had told you something, and you are sure it was God, then by all means stand on it and claim it. If he hasn't, then find out what he has in mind for you before claiming anything.

At times, we may need to ask God for discernment on where our guidance is coming from. It may be an evil person or spirit, if not God. Having people pray for your discernment can help you make wiser decisions.

How should we pray?

We need to persevere in our prayer. That is very important. It may mean more than a few minutes now and then.

When we choose to be an intercessor, we may accompany it with a fast and vigil, which is especially powerful for healing. Before fasting, we should consider our health and get a doctor's recommendation. Some people fast for a day, a meal, abstain from a favorite food, or just have bread and water.

When we pray for healing for ourselves and others, there may be no favorable results. That may be due to our need to repent of our sins.

Evil spirits may also interfere with a prayer request being answered with "yes." Our best course of action in this case is to take authority in the name of Jesus and learn how to cast out evil spirits. Then the situation will be open for the request to take place.

God is way ahead of us in his plans for our life.

Faith is evident when healing is about to occur. It's not wishful thinking or strenuous will power. It is not gritting your teeth. Instead, it is confident assurance concerning what we hope for and conviction about things we don't see.

If our request is granted, it may require follow-up on our part. The root causes of the problem must be cared for or the problem can come back. Root causes may be physical, psychological, or spiritual.

What we receive in faith needs to be maintained in faith. If, for example, we doubt that a healing has taken place, the healing will likely disappear.

Despite our perseverance in prayer, there will always be a limitation in our ministries. This is because paradise can't occur until Jesus comes again into fullness. Even the holiest of people struggled with problems that didn't go away. Yet despite their problems, God worked through them. St. Paul is a good example of one whose health problem persisted despite frequent prayer to have the affliction removed. He didn't let it hold him back, however. He worked around it and thrived.

Chapter 4
How Do I Pray?

We are asked to pray frequently which means to keep your thoughts filled with God. To simply say the word "God" or "Jesus" is a prayer. While doing everyday activities, you can think of Him. You could even say to yourself, "God is with me and I am with You," or "Your power is everywhere around me." You can praise him for things created everywhere around you.

Try to not just stay focused on prayers for your own needs. Pray enough prayers for other people for they will cling to you and transform your life. You can change the world through prayer. A case in point is the fall of communism giving way to democracy in a number of countries. That was the result of many prayers over the years.

Some people use time during their lunch hour at work to pray alone or with others. You can pray while you cook, eat, clean, drive, take a shower, etc.

The power of prayer is sent off through our brain's thoughts to other people. They may take a certain course of action because your prayer thoughts physically reached them in some unexplained way. Even people in trouble have been known to alert loved ones that they are in distress. We sometimes sense their silent communication to us, then take action.

Prayer can also bring inner joy and peace to us. It may also give outer joy into our lives over time.

With experience, we soon learn praying for our agenda versus God's can bring disappointments. With prayer, we surrender to God's purposes. God knows our needs before we ask Him. We don't have to use fancy speech when praying. Praying repetitious prayers without thought or feeling may not get us the results we feel we need.

Knowing what to pray is as important as knowing how to pray. Be inspired to see outcomes that give God the greatest glory, for that is a central purpose of prayer. An outcome that fails to give God the greatest glory may not necessarily be a miracle.

God wants us to develop a relationship with Him through our prayers, not simply call on him during times of requests and then hang up. Relationships limited to this kind of communication go downhill fast. The more fellowship we develop with God, the more we will know how to pray and what to pray.

Chapter 5
Prayer Life Guidelines

How Do I Pray?

Asking God to show us how he wants us to pray is a wise thing to do. We may even ask for the discernment of others on this matter.

One obstacle to answered prayers may be discouragement. The situation may get worse before our eyes. Learning to persevere is important in prayer. History is full of examples of people receiving a "yes" to a prayer request because they didn't give up.

An effective intercessor is one who simply makes a long-term decision to plead on behalf of another. Sometimes a person is unwilling or unable to pray for himself.

Scripture has even mentioned times when one person could have been an intercessor and saved people from harsh consequences. Ezekiel 22:30-31 is one example. It says, "Thus I have searched among them for someone who could build a wall or stand in the breach before me to keep me from destroying the land; but I found no one. Therefore, I have poured out my fury upon them; with my fiery wrath I have consumed them; I have brought down their conduct upon their heads, says the Lord God." When no one came forward, the people suffered, brought down by their own behavior. This shows how much value God places on intercession.

Applying an "instant results" mentality to our prayer can get us into trouble. We may not see quick results. God wants to change people, both the person praying, and the one being prayed for.

God wants everyone to be an intercessor. It is not an option he wants us to choose. It's a responsibility that comes hand in hand with the many benefits and pleasures of being God's children. Our schedules are never too busy for a few minutes of prayer.

When coming to the Lord as an intercessor, it's important, first of all, to repent of our own sins. Trying not to repeat the same sins shows God that we aren't just going through the motions with our words.

We need to pray not only as individuals, but as part of the larger community to which we belong, the body of Christ. When we do this, we show that we understand how we share in the painful consequences that others bring on the world. Moses is a good example of a biblical figure willing to stand in the gap totally, even suffering punishment, if God wanted to respond that way.

> "You have committed a grave sin," Moses told the people.
> "I will go up to the Lord; then perhaps I may be able to make atonement for your sin." So Moses went back to the Lord and said, "Ah, this people had indeed committed a grave sin in making a god of gold for themselves! If you would not only forgive their sin! If you will not, then strike me out of the book you have written." Ex. 32:30

The point is, we all share in the condition of the people of God. We may not approve of what's going on, and we may be blameless in a certain situation, yet we share in the responsibility of the good and bad that occurs in the world. Whenever we come to prayer, we are to come humbly, as sinners ourselves, begging for the mercy of God on us all. This allows us to pray according to God's mind. God will hear and answer our prayer.

Intercession is so important to the Lord that he sometimes provides intercessors for us that we don't even know. By all means, pray for whatever and whoever God calls you to pray for. Pray for our nation, family, community, and needs of the world.

When a person or topic comes to your mind, go to the Lord and say, "Lord, how do you want me to pray today?" Some people even set a special time and place it aside for this purpose. Try to be relatively free of distraction.

Chapter 6
Spiritual Reflections and Observations

Think and ponder the impossible . . . you're halfway to the solution.

When you visualize what you want to be, or own, etc., the opportunities will present themselves to make it possible.

A quote from *Earth Angels* book, page 51, by *Guideposts*. There are only two ways to live your life. One is as though nothing is a miracle. The other as though everything is a miracle.

Albert Einstein

God answers our prayer requests with either "yes" or "no" or "wait."

Sometimes an incident happens in our life that seems like a coincidence. It is not always for our sake. It may be for the benefit of another person. How did the coincidence impact someone else's life? Sometimes we'll find out, and other times not.

I'm sure that years ago, those willing to believe that the earth was a sphere and not flat were considered crazy. How could they prove this belief or insight that they had? Eventually, God found ways for it to be proven.

Find a niche that needs filling. Do it better and, if others have a similar niche, help keep customers satisfied.

Everyday aggravations and inconveniences can spark ideas in you for new products and services.

Look inside and find what you <u>can</u> do.

It's tragic to have no goals to reach for.

Ask God to inspire you with goals that you'll find rewarding to achieve as well as character-building to achieve.

Tragedy often brings about needed changes in a situation. We often ignore or overlook a potential problem until tragedy occurs.

Moving out of an emotional rut is hard when we aren't forgiving of someone.

When we are having trouble forgiving someone, we may ask God to help us in that process. His main concern is that we are willing to do it, even if it takes time.

Sometimes when we are hurt by someone, we want them to suffer just as deeply as they have made us suffer. We see it as a form of justice. Yet they may have asked God's forgiveness and received it. Their suffering may be little if any due to their wrongdoing. Sometimes this can infuriate us. Strangely enough, we dare to ask for God's mercy and forgiveness for ourselves.

People who are of a forgiving nature are usually a lot happier than those who aren't.

Sometimes we get what we asked for, and we're still unhappy.

We will continue to find better solutions for the same problems.

It's just as easy to ask for more as it is to ask for less.

Confessing your sins and failures to God starts the healing process for you and can also help a prayer request to turn out favorably. It gets rid of guilt and shame.

Be thankful for things that God blesses you and others with. This is crucial.

How much tithing and giving what you have to others is enough? Some groups say 10%, others don't restrict it to a formula. They just say look to your heart. God is mysterious in how he wants us to interpret his word. People over the centuries have used scripture to mean whatever their agenda needs. Both good and bad people use scripture for their purposes.

Tithing can be your free time if you income is more limited. Time is worth money for many kinds of services that people pay for.

God helps us first to believe in our dream, then watch it as it becomes an achievement. We may do the work ourselves, or find others' help to turn it into reality.

My motto as a child and adult was always think big and pray big. My results kept me using that approach.

Robert Kennedy was quoted, saying, "Some see things as they are and ask, 'why?' others dream things that never were and ask, 'why not?'

If you prayed for some of my requests too, then let's face it, there's strength in numbers.

You can make a big difference in the world without fame or fortune. Prayer does it without a doubt. You can pray openly with others or privately without anyone knowing about your dialogue with God.

Anyone, even a child, can make a huge impact in another person's life through his or her prayer requests. We can all practice small acts of kindness that will make a difference in people's lives.

No matter how farfetched your idea is or your request, just keep telling yourself, "anything's possible with God."

Hanging in there and having perseverance can bring about a desired goal. If it's not a wise goal for us personally to take, perseverance may not bring desired results. Ask God for wisdom on what path to take.

We may have a number of purposes in life, and therefore, a number of struggles may occur that help us discover our purposes.

The most inconspicuous or lowly person you encounter in life can be your meal ticket to success in various areas of your life. God takes prayers of all well-meaning people seriously. He judges requests by different standards than people do. He loves us all and wants to help us all.

When I started to remember past times when God answered a request with "yes," it gave me patience and determination with new requests.

I often get my best ideas when I'm relaxed and not trying hard to come up with a good idea. What sounds impossible to me is not impossible with God.

Don't be afraid to ask God for more. It's just as easy as asking for less.

As I remember my requests answered with "yes," I started to feel like these truths were stranger than fiction.

One person can make a world of difference. With God, we are all equal in His eyes. He'll do amazing things for anybody.

Letting go and letting God is important. Have just enough faith that He'll do it if it's a good idea, and what he does may boggle your mind.

Our prayer requests are part of a mosaic that makes all kinds of good things happen. Without these requests, perhaps a number of good situations wouldn't have occurred. Prayer and the action of others and/or ourselves brings amazing results for all kinds of things.

People can say God cares or people can show God cares.

It's hard to care about the soul when the body is neglected.

People are less likely to give up on God during difficult times when other people are there for them all the way.

So often our fears are realized because they stay on our minds too often and the forces of nature are then set in motion for them to happen. The same can hold true for our hopes and dreams of better things. They too can be attracted to us by our fearless and vigilant hope.

Our neglect of our body is all too often a symptom of our neglect of our spiritual life too.

Mary Ardissone

God uses people to show he cares about us.

Praying doesn't only happen when we address God by name during our request or in thanking Him.

Sometimes our taking action, rather than praying for a purpose, is the best answer to someone's prayer request. If we pass the buck, God has to search for another willing person.

God's answer to our prayer is often a process.

God's answer to prayer can be "yes," "no," or "wait."

Getting a "yes" answer to a prayer request may involve waiting a short time or a long time.

God may try to do something different than that which we ask. It may be done in a different method than we ask in order to accomplish more purposes.

God answers all prayers.

Prayer may be used to get us in touch with reality. By praying for only a miracle, we may be avoiding the need to face what's happening in our life.

God only wants what is best for us, yet He will let us make mistakes to help us learn. We may need more information to help us solve a problem.

There are times when we may accomplish more good for someone by speaking to God about the person than by speaking to the person about God.

God is willing to show mercy and intervention if we ask Him.

Our biggest struggle may be not in obtaining God's forgiveness, but in forgiving ourselves.

We may struggle in not wanting God to be merciful to others, and yet to be merciful to us in our failings.

Our ability to have successful relationships with others and attracting desirable people may hinge on our forgiveness of ourselves and others for the failings that we have.

We are blessed so that we may be a blessing to others. We are healed so that we can help others.

Your small or hidden ministry can often make the biggest difference.

All ministries matter because we all are dependent on each other to function.

Each of us was designed by God to be unique. We were shaped to do certain things.

You are the way you are because God wants you to be active in a specific kind of service.

Everything that happens in our life is significant. God uses all of it to shape you for the service you'll be able to provide to others and to Him.

We instinctively care about some things more than others. These are clues for you on where you should be serving. God doesn't want you to waste your life doing mostly boring activities.

The nature of our heart is revealed in what we do and don't feel passionate about.

Our interests come from God so that we can fulfill his purposes. Don't ignore your interests. There are reasons why you enjoy pursuing certain things.

We do better at things we feel passionate about and enjoy doing. It can explain job losses, even our self sabotage or God's hand in it may be present.

If enthusiasm is present, it's a sign that we're serving God from our heart. Being effective is also a sign that we're serving God from our heart.

Aim to serve God in a way that expresses your heart.

Mary Ardissone

Try to find out what you love to do, what you were given the heart to do, then do it for God's glory.

What do you do for sheer enjoyment? What do you do without being nagged to do it?

We're all born with natural talents.

We all have abilities, some of them even dormant and untapped, waiting to be discovered and used.

Some studies have revealed that we have as many as 500 to 700 different skills and abilities, far more than any of us realize.

Determine what you are and aren't good at.

Only dedicate your life to tasks you have a talent for and like to do.

God matches our calling and our capabilities.

God loves variety and made each one of us unique.

Some of us are introverts, others are extroverts. Some love routine, other variety. Some people tend to be thinkers and others feelers. Some work best in a team and others work best when given an individual assignment.

Variety gives balance to the world.

Our life experiences, many beyond our control, have shaped us. God molds us this way for his purposes.

God never wastes our hurtful experiences. Often our greatest service to others will come out of our greatest hurt.

We are comforted in our painful experiences so that we can provide the same comfort to others. Even the experiences we regret and want to hide can be used to help others.

For our most painful experiences to be used by God, we must share them with others. It also helps heal us.

Showing how God's grace has helped us during times of weakness encourages others more than bragging about out strong points.

You'll be more successful when you pursue your abilities and spiritual gifts in a way that best expresses your personality and experiences.

Focus on talents God has given <u>you</u> to use rather than talents of other people.

Avoid trying to serve God in ways that you aren't equipped to ever serve Him. It is a waste of your time, talent, and energy.

To discover what your talents are, take a long look at what you're good at and what you're not good at. Others will often confirm your natural abilities and spiritual gifts.

Ask yourself where you've already been successful.

A great way to discover gifts and abilities that you have is to experiment with various areas of service. If you start to see results and the confirmation of others, then you know you are talented in that area.

If you avoid experimenting with different areas, you will not discover your various talents. You're never too old to experiment with a new area.

Questions to ask yourself about using a talent:

—What do I enjoy doing the most?
—During what activity do I feel most fully alive?
—Do I lose track of time during a particular activity?
—Do I enjoy routine or variety?
—Do I prefer serving by myself or as part of a team?
—Am I introverted or extroverted?
—Do I tend to be a thinker or a feeler?
—Do I enjoy competing or cooperating most?

We seldom will see God's good plan in failure or pain or embarrassment while it is happening. However, in hindsight, we will often see how God has intended a problem for good.

Mary Ardissone

God wants us to take the lessons we've learned to help others.

Recognize your limitations, since nobody is good at everything.

We all have defined roles. We experience stress when we try to overextend ourselves for service.

We need to avoid comparing our God-given form of service to that of others.

When we conform our service to the expectations of others, it's to lose joy in doing it.

Comparing our tasks and the results of them should not be compared with anyone else. The reason is simple. We will always be able to find someone who seems to do the job much better than us. This leads to discouragement.

There are also others who don't perform as well at a task and comparing ourselves to them will eventually rob us of the joy in doing it.

If you don't exercise your talents and abilities, they will weaken. You can also lose them.

When you use your abilities, God will increase them.

Practice helps our abilities to improve and be enlarged. Take advantage of training opportunities to develop your skills.

God is served when we serve others.

God determines your greatness by the number of people you are serving, not how many serve you.

Your primary area of service should be where your talents and abilities lie. The secondary area of service is wherever you are needed at the time. An accident scene could be one example.

A real servant does what's needed, even when it's inconvenient for him. He doesn't become resentful when God interrupts a plan for some other activity. These interruptions can be seen as God's appointments for service and the goal is to be happy doing them.

An effective servant is always on the lookout for ways to help others. In business settings, these people are more likely to keep customers happy.

Due to insensitivity, we may miss various occasions to serve others. Once the chance passes, it may never return again.

If you wait for perfect conditions, you will never get anything done. Ecclesiastes 11:4.

It is better to have less-than-perfect service than the best intention.

We all start out by doing things in less than perfect ways.

Part of our character curriculum is to do mundane things as well as interesting things.

Effective servants finish their tasks and keep their promises. They are dependable and trustworthy.

None of us retires from serving God.

Some goals that we strive for are fulfillment, satisfaction, and fruitfulness. You achieve all three of these things when you serve in a way that is consistent with the personality that God has given you.

There are short-term solutions and long-term solutions. The more we learn about a subject, the more likely we are to come up with a long-term solution that will work out.

We don't always get everything our heart desires, yet God is generous and will answer prayers with wisdom, whatever is good for the long haul. Always be thankful when a request is answered with a "yes."

With God, the door is always open. He's always there to listen to your wishes, hopes, and concerns.

When we read about the true experiences of others, we are inclined to think, "That could be me," or "I wish it were me," or "Hey, that is me!"

Mary Ardissone

Some helpful virtues to have when praying are faith, hope, patience, and confidence that only the best answer will happen.

God hears our needs and desires, even when we don't address him by name when we express them.

When you're at the bottom of the heap and have nothing to offer but yourself, you'll quickly find out who your real friends are.

God sees your potential even when you don't see it yourself.

Answers are everywhere that we're open for them to be.

Sometimes an incident happens in our life that seems like a coincidence. It's not always for our sake. It may be for the benefit of another person. How did the coincidence impact someone else's life? Sometimes we'll find out, and other times not.

Our dreams are the reality of the future. We all have the ability to make a difference.

Somebody believed in the idea just as much as you did and was praying for you to succeed at it.

God will give you the power to achieve his purpose. If you dream it, believe in it, you can achieve it.

If you're thinking small, it's you. If you're thinking large, it's God.

God give me a dream that you planned for my life and the wisdom and perseverance to go after it and achieve it.

When pacing your progress on a goal, the challenge is to know when to move forward, hold back, dig in, yield, hold on, let go, plan alone or form a partnership. Look to God as the all-wise timekeeper. He'll help you make the correct move, in the best way, at the right time. Ask God for wisdom as you pace yourself. Positive thinkers avoid quitting, they simply change their pace to win the race.

Launching a new idea takes faith, despite the risks involved. Unexpected elements keep us on our toes. God doesn't let us become so smart that we become absolutely confident that we will be successful with our new creations. Ask God for the courage to be creative since it is always the ultimate act of believing.

Moving ahead in unchartered territory calls for faith. But faith manages the risks responsibly. It takes wise and cautious maneuvering. A road up a mountain is rarely a straight path. The road will wind and curve. The detour may go on for miles before a "switch-back" can be executed and you can then start moving in on your destination again. Be willing to exercise patience rather than reckless impulsiveness.

In order to move ahead toward a goal, meditation must be translated into creative activity. The actions may be small, but move forward just the same. It may mean picking up the telephone or reaching for a pen or pencil. Maybe you need to hit the books, make contacts and communicate. Selling yourself and your ideas may be necessary. Avoid waiting for God to drop miracles out of a cloud. Start to work by doing the most difficult job first. You'll look back at the day and know you've made progress.

Look for opportunities and possibilities for personal growth that you can work on tomorrow. Perhaps there's a virtue that needs to be worked on. To be satisfied with the status quo in any area of life will cause eventual decline and eventually hurts the human spirit. Grow with the possibilities of tomorrow.

To renew your strength during difficult times, look at what you have left, not at what you lost. Realize what God has done for you such as forgiveness, healing, and redemption. He renews your strength and crowns you with loving kindness. List the other assets that you have often taken for granted such are your friends, citizenship, education, job, family. You'll see that the list of everything you have going for you is longer than you think. This can give you renewed strength.

Are there forces of sin and doubt that are placing demands on your spirit today? We can't always avoid negative storms. To brace yourself today with positive affirmations, remember the following:

— With God at your side, you can brace yourself for times of despair, temptation, doubt, and sin.
— God won't let you be defeated.

— A divine idea has been entrusted to you by God. Guard it with your eternal soul.

— Avoid taking your eye off the walk of faith.

— Realize that each storm will pass. Winter always turns to spring with God's help.

— Don't let your faith in God be abandoned. He always will allow the sun to rise tomorrow.

Counting your blessings strengthens your faith. It produces contentment even in the most difficult situations. As you recall times when you steered yourself around conflicts this year, remember that only God made it possible.

When faced with what seems like an unsolvable problem, consider the following approach. Make a list on paper of perhaps ten possible ways to accomplish the impossible problem. It doesn't matter how unlikely the solution is. Then list the first thoughts that come to your mind. You'll be surprised at how God will operate within you. If one comes from God, it will grab you and you won't be able to shake it. It will become part of the answer to the problem.

Try to understand what humility is and what it isn't. Let your light shine and try complimenting yourself each day when you pray. Realize that you have abilities and gifts that you can use. Healthy humility can give you a healthy inner glow.

One way that you can see the reality of miracles in your everyday life is by realizing that you are a survivor of survivors. Your life is an unbroken genetic string that goes back to the beginning of man. Your existence wasn't ended by war, famine, a plague, an accident, or a crime. You're a good person to spread God's love around the world each day.

Climbing your way out of a difficult action requires more than prayer. It requires action and work. Faith is working as well as believing.

You may find yourself surrounded by more opportunities than you can handle. First, list your daily possibilities on a sheet of paper. Make a list of things you could do today, should do today, and would like to do today.

Decide the basic objectives that you want to complete. Begin to prioritize the options by giving your best time to the project that is most important.

If you lack resources to take advantage of a great opportunity, do this. If you lack resources, carefully look for other positive thinkers that you can approach with your project. Share the opportunity with the potential profit before you abandon the project for lack of time or money. This can be called "setting up limited partnerships."

Before you begin, form and pursue an unlimited partnership with God as you think, plan, and dream together.

We can ask God to show us how He wants us to pray for ourselves and others. We may, at times, ask for the discernment of others for how we should pray.

When we pray for months, even years for an intention, we may still not receive a final answer to it. We wonder if we're praying correctly for it. Be humble and open before God. He will show us how to pray in his name so that our intercession will be heard.

An obstacle to answered prayer can be discouragement. Sometimes after praying for weeks or months, we see no change and want to give up. We may see the situation get worse before it gets better. Learning to persevere is important. History is full of examples of people who never gave up praying for a cause and were later pleased with the answer that God provided.

We are asked to be intercessors for others when praying. The dictionary defines to intercede as "to pray or petition God in behalf of another." Making a long-term commitment to plead on behalf of another is encouraged in scripture. Those having difficulty praying for themselves are helped by those praying for them. Even the prayers of one person were known in scripture to have the power to save a nation from harsh judgment.

Intercessory prayer is a role that can move mountains. It is unwise to apply an instant results mentality to our prayer. We may find that God is working in a different way because he wants change from people, both the intercessor and the one being prayed for. When we have expected instant results, we become discouraged and may want to give up. Intercession requires hard work, dedication, and perseverance on our part.

We are all called to intercession by God. Our schedules are never too busy for a few minutes of prayer.

There are four requirements for an intercessor. The first requirement is repentance for our sins. We must be in a right place with God before expecting him to do all kinds of favors for us and for those being prayed for. When we continue to repeat our same wrongdoings, it's often because we are not truly sorry in the first place and willing to change. We can always ask for help from God if we don't know how best to change patterns in our life. This makes greater personal joy, peace, and hope possible.

Joining others in prayer, not just as an isolated individual, is very helpful. We should also ask for God's mercy and forgiveness for all his people. This is commonly cited in scripture as a practice of the great spiritual leaders. They turned to God in prayer not as a judge and executioner, but as an intercessor, for they too knew they were sinners in their own right. This humble way of prayer opened up their minds to God's influence, and he then heard and answered their prayer. Self-righteousness has always been discouraged.

What does God want us to pray for? Think of the needs of family members, your church, and in the world. We need to ask him how to pray for our nation, family, community, and the needs of the world.

Next, decide on the time of the week you plan to set aside for intercession. It's important that you remain relatively free of distraction.

Some people use fasting during a special period of prayer requests to show God just how serious they are and that they want God to hear their prayer. Ask for wisdom on this point since no two people's health and work situation are the same. For some, it is an unwise decision to fast completely. Abstaining from dessert may be a form of fasting for some.

Why not be one who intervenes in your family, community, and nation, and the world. It can make the lives of those touched by your prayers better and your own as well. Ask others to pray for you too.

Thanking God in all answers he provides is also important. We have to realize that in the large long-term scheme of things, our desired answer will not always be best for us and those we pray for. Trying to be one with God makes us more understanding of the answer he provides for us.

As we look back on our lives, if we always received a "yes" to each request we made of God, others that benefited us couldn't have eventually happened.

NOTES

www.ingramcontent.com/pod-product-compliance
Lightning Source LLC
Chambersburg PA
CBHW071539080526
44588CB00011B/1726